Mastering ETFs

Unleashing the Potential of

Exchange-Traded Funds (ETFs) for

Successful Investing

Copyright © 2023

by Luke Harrington

All rights reserved. No part of this book may be reproduced or used in any manner without written permission of the copyright owner except for the use of quotations in a book review.

Table of Content

Introduction

Evolution and Growth of ETFs: From Inception to Prominence

Structure of ETFs: A Basket of Possibilities

Diversification within a Single Investment: The Power of ETFs

Types of ETFs: From Broad-Based to Specialized Strategies

Benefits of ETFs: A Comparative Analysis

Benefits of ETFs: Diversification and Risk Management: Harnessing Portfolio Efficiency

Trading ETFs on Stock Exchanges

Various Tools for Evaluating ETFs: Indicators and Metrics

Historical Performance Indicators

Risk Assessment Metrics

Top 10 ETFs: Exploring Diverse Investment Opportunities

Introduction

As we embark on a journey into the world of Exchange-Traded Funds (ETFs), it is crucial to grasp the essence of these financial instruments.

In this opening chapter, we will lay the foundation by providing a clear definition of ETFs and highlighting their distinguishing features. ETFs, often hailed as hybrid investment instruments, possess a unique blend of characteristics that combine the advantages of both mutual funds and individual stocks. We will explore the remarkable flexibility, transparency, and tradability that set ETFs apart from traditional investment options, ultimately unlocking their potential as a powerful tool for investors seeking diversification, liquidity, and cost efficiency.

To understand ETFs, we must first grasp their fundamental nature and how they differ from other investment vehicles.

The Convergence of Mutual Funds and Individual Stocks: ETFs occupy a distinctive space in the investment landscape, bridging the gap between mutual funds and individual stocks. While mutual funds pool investors' funds to create a diversified portfolio, ETFs combine this diversification aspect with the tradability and flexibility of individual stocks. This fusion creates an investment vehicle that offers the best of both worlds.

Flexibility: Embracing a Range of Investment Strategies

One of the standout features of ETFs is their remarkable flexibility. These instruments are designed to track an underlying index or asset class, giving investors exposure to a broad range of securities within a single trade. ETFs provide access to various investment strategies, including broad-based indices, sector-specific themes, geographic regions, and even niche areas such as commodities or specific market factors. This flexibility allows investors to align their investment choices with their risk appetite, investment goals, and market views.

Transparency: Clear Insight into Holdings and Performance

Transparency is a crucial aspect of ETFs that sets them apart from many other investment options. Unlike traditional mutual funds, which disclose their holdings periodically, ETFs provide daily transparency regarding their portfolio compositions. This level of transparency allows investors to understand the underlying securities held by the ETF, assess the risks associated with those securities, and evaluate the fund's performance. This transparency empowers investors with the necessary information to make informed decisions and actively manage their portfolios.

Tradability: Harnessing the Power of Exchange Trading

The tradability of ETFs on stock exchanges is a significant advantage that distinguishes them from other investment vehicles. ETFs can be bought and sold throughout the trading day at market prices, just like individual stocks. This intraday liquidity allows investors to enter or exit positions swiftly, responding to market conditions and capitalizing on investment opportunities. The ability to trade ETFs in real-time empowers investors to exercise greater control over their investment strategies, enhancing their agility in a dynamic market environment.

Exploring the Advantages of ETFs

Understanding the key features of ETFs provides the groundwork for appreciating the advantages they offer to investors.

Flexibility: Tailoring Portfolios to Individual Needs

The flexibility of ETFs enables investors to construct portfolios that align with their specific investment objectives and preferences. With a vast array of ETF options available, investors can choose from broad-based market indices, sector-specific ETFs, bond ETFs, or even those focused on specific investment strategies like dividend yield or low volatility. This ability to customize portfolios ensures that investors have the necessary tools to adapt to changing market conditions and optimize their risk-return profiles.

Transparency: Enhanced Visibility and Informed Decision-Making

The transparency of ETFs provides investors with clear visibility into the underlying holdings and performance of the fund. By knowing the securities in which they are investing, investors can conduct thorough analysis, assess the risks, and evaluate the alignment of the ETF with their investment goals. This transparency fosters informed decision-making, allowing investors to allocate their capital wisely and maintain confidence in their investment choices.

Tradability: Seizing Opportunities in Real-Time

The tradability of ETFs on stock exchanges offers a level of liquidity and convenience that is unparalleled in traditional investment vehicles. Investors can execute trades for ETFs throughout the trading day, taking advantage of intraday price movements and swiftly responding to market developments. This real-time tradability empowers investors to implement their investment strategies effectively, including tactical allocation, risk management, and opportunistic trading, all with the ease and efficiency offered by exchange trading.

This chapter lay the groundwork for our exploration into the world of ETFs. ETFs are a convergence of mutual funds and individual stocks, highlighting their flexibility, transparency, and tradability as key distinguishing features. By combining the benefits of diversification, adaptability, and liquidity, ETFs offer investors a powerful tool to construct well-tailored portfolios and navigate the complexities of financial markets.

As we delve deeper into the world of ETFs, we will uncover the nuances of their structure, types, trading mechanisms, and the diverse range of investment opportunities they present.

Evolution and Growth of ETFs: From Inception to Prominence

Understanding the evolution of ETFs is essential for appreciating their significance in modern financial markets and the growing demand among investors. We will embark on a journey through time, exploring the milestones, regulatory changes, and market dynamics that have shaped the ETF landscape, transforming these instruments from nascent ideas to prominent investment vehicles.

Tracing the Origins of ETFs

To grasp the evolution of ETFs, we must delve into their historical development and understand the key factors that led to their emergence.

The Birth of Index Funds: A Foundation for ETFs

The roots of ETFs can be traced back to the introduction of index funds in the 1970s. Index funds, pioneered by John Bogle and his creation of the Vanguard 500 Index Fund, aimed to replicate the performance of a specific market index. These index funds provided investors with a cost-effective way to gain exposure to broad market indices, without the need for active stock selection.

Nathan Most and the Concept of ETFs

The idea of ETFs as we know them today was first proposed by Nathan Most in the early 1980s. Most envisioned an investment vehicle that could be traded like a stock but would provide investors with diversified exposure to a basket of securities. Although Most's concept did not come to fruition at the time, it laid the groundwork for the future development of ETFs.

The Launch of SPDR: The First ETF

The birth of the first ETF, known as the Standard & Poor's Depository Receipts (SPDR), marked a significant milestone in the evolution of ETFs. Introduced in 1993, SPDR sought to track the performance of the S&P 500 Index. This groundbreaking product, managed by State Street Global Advisors, offered investors a new way to access broad-based market exposure, combining the benefits of diversification and intraday

tradability.

The Rise of ETFs: Factors Driving Growth and Popularity

Regulatory Changes: Unlocking the Potential of ETFs

The growth of ETFs can be attributed, in part, to regulatory changes that facilitated their expansion. In 1996, the Securities and Exchange Commission (SEC) introduced Rule 6c-11, which streamlined the regulatory process for ETFs. This rule allowed ETFs to operate more efficiently, reducing the time and cost associated with launching new products. Furthermore, regulatory developments such as the granting of exemptive relief for custom basket ETFs opened doors for increased product innovation.

Advancements in Technology and Market Infrastructure

The growth of ETFs has been supported by advancements in technology and market infrastructure. The development of electronic trading platforms, such as the creation of the National Market System (NMS) in the United States, has facilitated the efficient trading of ETFs on stock exchanges. The proliferation of online brokerage platforms and the democratization of access to financial markets have also played a significant role in the increased adoption of ETFs among retail investors.

Market Dynamics: Meeting Investor Demands

The evolving needs of investors have also contributed to the growth and popularity of ETFs. Investors increasingly seek cost-effective, transparent, and flexible investment solutions that provide diversification and liquidity. ETFs, with their low expense ratios, transparent holdings, and intraday tradability, have emerged as an attractive option for investors seeking to build diversified portfolios, implement specific investment strategies, and manage risk efficiently.

The Rise of Passive Investing: The rise of passive investing, where investors seek to replicate the performance of a specific market index rather than actively select individual securities, has propelled the growth of ETFs. As investors embrace the evidence supporting the long-term benefits of passive strategies, ETFs have become a preferred vehicle for gaining broad market exposure. The low costs associated with ETFs compared to actively managed mutual funds have further enhanced their appeal, as fees can eat into investors' returns over time.

We have traced the evolution of ETFs from their origins as a concept to their prominent position in modern financial markets. We explored the birth of index funds, the visionary ideas of Nathan Most, and the launch of the first ETF, SPDR. Regulatory changes, technological advancements, investor demands, and the rise of passive investing have all played pivotal roles in the growth and popularity of ETFs. Understanding the historical development of ETFs provides us with valuable insights into their significance as a powerful investment tool and sets the stage for our exploration of their structure, types, and trading mechanisms in the subsequent chapters of this book.

Structure of ETFs: A Basket of Possibilities

In this chapter, we will dig deep into the underlying structure of these innovative investment instruments. Understanding the structure of ETFs is crucial for investors to grasp the mechanics behind their creation, trading, and the unique benefits they offer. We will explore the role of Authorized Participants, the creation-redemption process, and how ETFs provide investors with exposure to a diversified portfolio of securities within a single investment. By unraveling the structure of ETFs, we unlock a world of possibilities for investors seeking efficient and flexible ways to navigate the

financial markets.

Understanding the Structure of ETFs

The Fundamentals: ETFs as Open-Ended Investment Companies

At their core, ETFs are open-ended investment companies that issue shares to investors. This structure allows ETFs to create and redeem shares based on investor demand, ensuring that the number of shares in circulation remains closely aligned with the value of the underlying assets.

Authorized Participants: The Key Players in ETF Creation

The creation of ETF shares involves a crucial role played by Authorized Participants (APs). APs are typically large financial institutions or market makers that have the authorization to create and redeem ETF shares. They facilitate the creation process by delivering a basket of underlying securities to the ETF provider in exchange for newly created ETF shares or vice versa.

Creation-Redemption Process: The Engine Behind ETF Efficiency

Creation of ETF Shares: Meeting Investor Demand

The creation process of ETF shares enables the continuous availability of shares in response to investor demand. When there is sufficient demand for new shares, APs work with the ETF provider to create new ETF shares. To do so, APs deliver a specified basket of underlying securities to the ETF provider, forming the basis of the newly created ETF shares. This process ensures that the number of shares in the ETF reflects the demand from investors.

Redemption of ETF Shares: Maintaining Balance and Liquidity

Conversely, when investors want to exit their positions in an ETF, the redemption process comes into play. APs can redeem ETF shares by returning a basket of underlying securities to the ETF provider in exchange for the corresponding ETF shares. This mechanism allows for efficient liquidation of ETF shares, ensuring that the ETF's share supply remains in line with investor demand.

In-Kind Creation and Redemption: Minimizing Disruption and Taxes

A unique aspect of the creation-redemption process is that it typically occurs in-kind rather than in cash. This means that when APs create or redeem ETF shares, they exchange the underlying securities rather than using cash. This in-kind process minimizes the need for the ETF to maintain large cash reserves and reduces transaction costs, benefiting both the ETF provider and investors.

Diversification within a Single Investment: The Power of ETFs

Mirroring the Composition of an Index or Asset Class

One of the key features of ETFs is their ability to mirror the composition of a specific index or asset class. By doing so, ETFs provide investors with exposure to a diversified portfolio of securities within a single investment. For example, an ETF that tracks the

S&P 500 Index will hold a basket of stocks that aims to replicate the performance of that index. This allows investors to gain broad market exposure and participate in the performance of the underlying securities without individually owning each stock.

Benefits of Diversification: Risk Reduction and Market Participation

The diversification offered by ETFs plays a crucial role in managing investment risk. By holding a diversified basket of securities, ETFs can reduce the impact of individual security performance on the overall portfolio. This risk reduction is especially valuable in volatile market conditions. Additionally, through their diversified holdings, ETFs provide investors with the opportunity to participate in the overall performance of a market segment or asset class, capturing broad market trends and potential growth opportunities.

We have explored the structure of ETFs and uncovered the mechanisms that drive their efficiency and flexibility. We discussed the role of Authorized Participants in the creation and redemption process, highlighting their significance in maintaining the balance and liquidity of ETFs. The creation-redemption process, conducted in-kind, minimizes disruption and transaction costs while optimizing tax efficiency.

Moreover, we explored how ETFs offer investors exposure to a diversified portfolio of securities within a single investment, mirroring the composition of an index or asset class. This enables investors to enjoy the benefits of diversification, risk reduction, and market participation. Understanding the structure of

ETFs sets the stage for deeper exploration into their various types, trading mechanisms, and the unique investment opportunities they provide.

Types of ETFs: From Broad-Based to Specialized Strategies

ETFs offer a wide range of investment opportunities, allowing investors to align their investment objectives with the appropriate fund. We will discuss broad-based ETFs that track major market indices, sector-specific ETFs that focus on specific industries or themes, and specialized ETFs that offer exposure to alternative asset classes such as commodities or currencies. By understanding the different types of ETFs, investors can tailor their portfolios to match their specific investment preferences and strategies.

Broad-Based ETFs: Tracking Major Market Indices

1.1 S&P 500 ETFs: Capturing the Performance of the U.S. Stock Market

Broad-based ETFs that track major market indices, such as the S&P 500, offer investors exposure to a diversified portfolio of stocks representing a broad segment of the U.S. stock market. These ETFs provide a convenient way for investors to gain broad market exposure and participate in the performance of the overall market.

1.2 Global Market ETFs: Accessing International Markets

Global market ETFs allow investors to diversify their portfolios beyond domestic markets by providing exposure to international equity markets. These ETFs may track indices such as the MSCI World Index or regional indices like the FTSE Developed Europe Index, enabling investors to access a wide range of international markets.

Sector-Specific ETFs: Focusing on Specific Industries or Themes

Technology Sector ETFs: Investing in Innovation

Sector-specific ETFs focus on specific industries or themes, allowing investors to gain targeted exposure to sectors that align with their investment outlook. Technology sector ETFs, for example, concentrate on companies involved in technology-related activities, providing investors with a way to participate in the growth potential of the technology sector.

Healthcare Sector ETFs: Capitalizing on the Health Industry

Healthcare sector ETFs focus on companies within the healthcare industry, including pharmaceuticals, biotechnology, and healthcare services. These ETFs allow investors to capitalize on the ongoing advancements in medical technologies and the potential growth of the healthcare sector.

Environmental, Social, and Governance (ESG) ETFs: Investing with a Conscience

ESG-focused ETFs incorporate environmental, social, and

governance factors into their investment strategies. These ETFs aim to align investors' values with their investments by selecting companies that adhere to sustainable and socially responsible practices. ESG ETFs provide a way for investors to support companies with positive environmental and social impact while seeking financial

returns.

Specialized ETFs: Exploring Alternative Asset Classes

Commodity ETFs: Accessing the

Commodities Market

Commodity ETFs offer investors

exposure to commodities such as

gold, oil, or agricultural products.

These ETFs enable investors to

participate in commodity price movements without the need for direct ownership or physical delivery of the underlying commodities.

Currency ETFs: Navigating the Foreign Exchange Market

Currency ETFs provide investors with exposure to foreign currencies, allowing them to diversify their currency holdings or capitalize on potential currency movements. These ETFs track the performance of currency pairs and can be used to hedge against currency risk or speculate on currency exchange rate fluctuations.

Alternative Asset Class ETFs: Diversifying Beyond Traditional Investments

Alternative asset class ETFs offer exposure to non-traditional investments, such as real estate, infrastructure, or private equity. These ETFs provide investors with the opportunity to diversify their portfolios and potentially benefit from alternative sources of return. Broad-based ETFs allow investors to gain exposure to major market indices, providing a convenient way to participate in the overall market. Sector-specific ETFs focus on specific industries or themes, enabling investors to align their portfolios with their investment outlook. Specialized ETFs offer exposure to alternative asset classes, allowing investors to diversify beyond traditional investments. By understanding the different types of ETFs, investors can select the funds that align with their investment objectives and strategies, and construct a well-rounded and diversified portfolio. The availability of a wide range of ETFs provides investors with the flexibility and opportunities to customize their investment approach according to their unique preferences and goals.

Benefits of ETFs: A Comparative Analysis

While both ETFs and mutual funds are popular investment vehicles, ETFs possess unique characteristics that make them appealing to a wide range of investors. We will compare ETFs to mutual funds and highlight the advantages of ETFs in terms of flexibility, cost efficiency, and tax considerations. By understanding the benefits of ETFs, investors can make informed decisions when constructing their investment portfolios.

Flexibility: Trading and Investment Options

Intraday Trading: The Ability to Trade Throughout the Day

One of the key advantages of ETFs over mutual funds is their intraday trading feature. ETFs can be bought and sold throughout the trading day at market prices, allowing investors to take advantage of market fluctuations and execute trades when desired. This flexibility provides investors with greater control over their investment decisions and the ability to respond quickly to market events.

Investment Strategies: Leveraged, Inverse, and Enhanced ETFs

ETFs offer a wide range of investment strategies beyond traditional long-only exposure. Leveraged ETFs aim to provide amplified returns based on the performance of an underlying index, while inverse ETFs seek to profit from declining markets. Enhanced ETFs incorporate strategies such as active management or factor-based investing to potentially enhance returns. These options give investors the opportunity to implement specific investment strategies that align with their risk tolerance and market outlook.

Cost Efficiency: Lower Expense Ratios

Expense Ratios: Comparing ETFs and Mutual Funds

Expense ratios represent the annual costs associated with owning an investment fund. ETFs typically have lower expense ratios compared to mutual funds, primarily due to their passive investment strategies and lower operating costs. This cost efficiency is advantageous for investors as it reduces the impact of fees on overall investment returns.

Transparency: Understanding Costs and Holdings

ETFs offer transparency regarding their underlying holdings and associated costs. Investors can easily access information about the composition of the ETF's portfolio, enabling them to make informed investment decisions. Additionally, ETFs' transparent structure allows investors to assess the impact of fees on their investments and make cost-conscious choices.

Tax Considerations: Potential for Greater Efficiency

Creation-Redemption Process: Tax Benefits of In-Kind Transactions

The creation-redemption process, unique to ETFs, provides potential tax advantages. By conducting in-kind transactions with Authorized Participants, ETFs can minimize taxable events. When investors redeem shares, the ETF provider can transfer the underlying securities, thus potentially avoiding capital gains distributions that typically occur with mutual funds.

This tax efficiency can enhance after-tax returns for investors.

Capital Gains Control: Individual Control over Tax Liabilities

ETFs also offer investors greater control over their capital gains tax liabilities. Since ETF shares are traded on exchanges, investors can choose when to sell their shares and potentially manage their capital gains exposure. In contrast, mutual funds distribute capital gains to all shareholders, regardless of individual redemption activity.

The ability to trade ETFs throughout the trading day at market prices provides investors with increased control and responsiveness. ETFs typically have lower expense ratios compared to mutual funds, reducing the impact of fees on investment returns. Moreover, the creation-redemption process of ETFs offers potential tax efficiency, allowing investors to minimize taxable events and potentially enhance after-tax returns. By understanding the benefits of ETFs, investors can make informed decisions when constructing their portfolios and capitalize on the advantages that ETFs offer in their investment journey.

Benefits of ETFs: Diversification and Risk Management: Harnessing Portfolio Efficiency

Diversification is a fundamental strategy for managing risk and optimizing returns in investment portfolios. By providing exposure to a broad range of securities, including domestic and international equities, fixed income assets, and other asset classes, ETFs offer investors the opportunity to build well-diversified portfolios that can mitigate risk and potentially enhance returns. We will explore the benefits of diversification and risk management through ETFs and discuss how investors can leverage these tools to achieve their investment objectives.

The Importance of Diversification

Understanding Diversification: Spreading Risk Across Assets

Diversification is a risk management technique that involves spreading investments across different assets or asset classes. By diversifying their portfolios, investors aim to reduce the impact of any single investment's performance on the overall portfolio. Diversification helps to minimize the exposure to idiosyncratic risk and increase the potential for consistent returns.

Benefits of Diversification: Mitigating Risk and Enhancing Returns

Diversification allows investors to reduce the volatility of their portfolios by spreading risk across different assets with potentially low or negative correlations. This strategy can help smooth out portfolio returns and reduce the potential for large losses. Additionally, diversification can enhance returns by capturing the performance of different market segments and asset classes.

Leveraging ETFs for Portfolio Diversification

Broad Market ETFs: Capturing the Performance of Major Indices

Broad market ETFs that track major indices, such as the S&P 500 or the MSCI World Index, provide investors with exposure to a diversified portfolio of stocks representing a broad segment of the market. These ETFs offer an efficient way to gain broad market exposure and participate in the performance of the overall market.

International ETFs: Expanding the Investment Universe

International ETFs allow investors to diversify their portfolios beyond domestic markets by providing exposure to international equity markets. These ETFs can track regional indices or focus on specific countries or regions, enabling investors to access a wide range of international markets and capture the potential growth opportunities they offer.

Fixed Income ETFs: Balancing Risk with Income Generation

Fixed income ETFs provide exposure to a diversified portfolio of bonds and other fixed income securities. These ETFs offer investors the opportunity to balance the risk in their portfolios by including fixed income assets that generate income and potentially act as a buffer during periods of market volatility.

Sector-Specific and Thematic ETFs: Targeted Exposure with Diversification

Sector-specific and thematic ETFs allow investors to gain targeted exposure to specific industries, themes, or market segments. These

ETFs can provide diversification within a specific sector or capitalize on emerging trends or investment themes. By combining sector-specific or thematic ETFs with broad market ETFs, investors can achieve a balance between targeted exposure and overall diversification.

Risk Management with ETFs

Risk Mitigation: Spreading Risk Across Asset Classes

ETFs offer investors the opportunity to spread risk across different asset classes beyond traditional equity investments. By including ETFs that provide exposure to fixed income assets, commodities, real estate, or alternative investments, investors can diversify their portfolios and potentially reduce the impact of any single asset class's performance on their overall portfolio.

Hedging Strategies: Mitigating Specific Risks

Certain ETFs, such as inverse ETFs or options-based ETFs, can be used as hedging tools to mitigate specific risks in a portfolio. Inverse ETFs aim to profit from declining markets, providing a potential hedge against market downturns. Options-based ETFs use options strategies to manage risk and potentially generate income. ETFs offer investors a convenient and efficient way to build well-diversified portfolios across different asset classes, including equities, fixed income, and other alternatives. By providing exposure to a broad range of securities, ETFs enable investors to spread risk and potentially enhance returns through diversification. Additionally, ETFs offer flexibility in accessing international markets, sector-specific exposure, and hedging strategies for risk management. By leveraging the benefits of diversification and risk management through ETFs, investors can strive to optimize their portfolios and achieve their investment objectives in an increasingly dynamic and complex financial landscape.

Trading ETFs on Stock Exchanges

ETFs provide investors with the flexibility to buy and sell shares throughout the trading day, offering intraday liquidity and accessibility. Understanding the process of trading ETFs on stock exchanges is crucial for investors to efficiently execute their investment strategies and take advantage of market opportunities. We will explore the key concepts of exchange trading, the role of market makers, the primary and secondary markets for ETFs, and the benefits of ETFs' intraday liquidity.

Understanding Exchange Trading

Liquidity: The Foundation of Exchange Trading

Liquidity refers to the ease with which an asset can be bought or sold in the market without significantly impacting its price. ETFs, being listed on stock exchanges, benefit from the liquidity provided by the exchange environment. Liquidity is crucial for investors as it ensures the ability to enter and exit positions at desired prices.

Accessibility: Trading ETFs on Stock Exchanges

ETFs can be bought and sold on stock exchanges through brokerage accounts, similar to individual stocks. This accessibility allows investors to participate in ETF trading using familiar platforms and order types, such as market orders, limit orders, or stop orders. Investors can place trades during regular trading hours and take advantage of real-time price information.

Mechanics of Trading ETFs on Stock Exchanges

Market Makers: Facilitating Liquidity and Efficient Trading

Market makers play a crucial role in ensuring liquidity and efficient trading for ETFs. These specialized participants commit to providing liquidity by offering to buy or sell ETF shares on the exchange. Market makers help narrow bid-ask spreads, ensuring that investors can trade ETFs at prices close to their underlying net asset value (NAV).

This continuous presence of market makers enhances market liquidity and allows investors to execute trades with minimal price impact.

Primary Market: Creation and Redemption Process

The primary market is where new ETF shares are created or existing shares are redeemed. Authorized

Participants, typically large financial institutions, play a key role in this process. Through the creation-redemption mechanism, Authorized Participants exchange a basket of underlying securities with the ETF provider in exchange for ETF shares. This process ensures that the supply of ETF shares remains in line with investor demand and helps keep the ETF's market price close to its NAV.

Secondary Market: Trading ETF Shares on Exchanges

The secondary market is where most individual investors participate in ETF trading. On stock exchanges, investors can buy and sell ETF shares from other market participants, including other individual investors, institutional investors, or market makers. ETFs trade like individual stocks, with their prices fluctuating throughout the trading day based on supply and demand dynamics. Investors can execute trades at prevailing market prices, allowing for real-time transactions and immediate exposure to the underlying securities held by the ETF.

Benefits of ETFs' Intraday Liquidity

Intraday Liquidity: Flexibility and Price Efficiency

ETFs' intraday liquidity is a significant advantage for investors. Unlike traditional mutual funds, which are priced once a day after the market close, ETFs can be bought or sold at any time during trading hours at prevailing market prices. This flexibility allows investors to respond quickly to market developments, news events, or changes in their investment strategies. Additionally, the ability to trade at market prices enhances price efficiency, ensuring that investors can transact at fair and transparent prices.

Market Orders and Limit Orders: Trading Strategies for ETFs

Investors have various trading strategies available when trading ETFs. Market orders are used to execute trades at the prevailing market price, providing immediate execution but potentially exposing investors to price fluctuations. Limit orders, on the other hand, allow investors to specify the maximum price they are willing to pay when buying or the minimum price they are willing to accept when selling ETF shares. Limit orders offer control over the execution price but may take longer to fill if the specified price is not reached.

Understanding the concepts of exchange trading, market makers, primary and secondary markets, and the benefits of intraday liquidity is crucial for investors seeking to efficiently execute their investment strategies using ETFs. The accessibility of ETFs on stock exchanges provides investors with the flexibility to buy and sell shares throughout the trading day, ensuring liquidity and enabling real-time exposure to the underlying securities. By leveraging the benefits of ETF trading, investors can effectively implement their investment decisions, respond to market dynamics, and take

advantage of opportunities in an

efficient and transparent manner.

Various Tools for Evaluating ETFs: Indicators and Metrics

As investors seek to make informed investment decisions, it becomes essential to analyze and assess the performance, risk, and other characteristics of ETFs. In this chapter, we will explore a range of indicators and metrics that can aid investors in evaluating ETFs effectively. These tools provide valuable insights into an ETF's historical performance, risk profile, liquidity, expense ratios, and tracking error, among other factors. By utilizing these tools, investors can gain a deeper understanding of ETFs and make informed decisions that align with their investment objectives.

Historical Performance Indicators

Total Return: Evaluating Long-Term Performance

Total return measures the overall performance of an ETF, considering both price appreciation and dividend or interest income. It provides investors with a comprehensive view of how an

ETF has performed over a specific period, accounting for capital gains and distributions.

Annualized Returns: Assessing Consistency and Growth

Annualized returns help investors gauge the average rate of return an ETF has generated annually over a specified period. This metric allows for the comparison of different ETFs and provides insights into their consistency and growth potential.

Risk Assessment Metrics

Standard Deviation: Measuring Volatility

Standard deviation measures the degree of price fluctuation or volatility experienced by an ETF. It provides insights into the potential risks associated with an investment and helps investors assess the level of price stability over a specific period.

Beta: Evaluating Sensitivity to Market Movements

Beta measures an ETF's sensitivity to market movements relative to a benchmark index. A beta greater than 1 indicates that the ETF tends to amplify market fluctuations, while a beta less than 1 suggests that the ETF is less volatile than the market.

Sharpe Ratio: Assessing Risk-Adjusted Returns

The Sharpe ratio evaluates an ETF's risk-adjusted returns by considering the excess return generated per unit of risk taken. It helps investors assess the efficiency of an ETF's returns relative to its volatility and provides insights into its risk-adjusted performance.

Liquidity and Trading Metrics

Average Daily Trading Volume: Assessing Liquidity

Average daily trading volume measures the average number of shares traded per day for an ETF. It serves as an indicator of liquidity, reflecting the ease with which investors can buy or sell ETF shares without significantly impacting their prices.

Bid-Ask Spread: Evaluating Transaction Costs

The bid-ask spread represents the difference between the highest price a buyer is willing to pay (bid) and the lowest price a seller is willing to accept (ask) for an ETF. A narrow bid-ask spread indicates higher liquidity and lower transaction costs for investors.

Expense and Cost Metrics

Expense Ratio: Evaluating Costs

The expense ratio reflects the annual operating expenses of an ETF, including management fees, administrative costs, and other expenses. A lower expense ratio indicates lower costs and can contribute to higher net returns for investors.

Tracking Error: Assessing Deviation from the Benchmark

Tracking error measures the extent to which an ETF's performance deviates from its benchmark index. A lower tracking error indicates that the ETF closely follows its underlying index, providing investors with more accurate performance representation.

We explored various tools for evaluating ETFs, including historical performance indicators, risk assessment metrics, liquidity and trading metrics, and expense and cost metrics. These tools provide investors with valuable insights into an ETF's performance, risk profile, liquidity, and cost efficiency. By utilizing these indicators and metrics, investors can make more informed decisions and align their investment strategies with their objectives. It is crucial for investors to conduct thorough evaluations and comparisons of ETFs to ensure that their investment choices align with their risk tolerance, return expectations,

and overall investment goals.

Top 10 ETFs: Exploring Diverse Investment Opportunities

We will explore the top 10 ETFs that offer diverse investment opportunities. These ETFs have been selected based on their popularity, asset size, track record, and their ability to provide exposure to different asset classes, sectors, or investment strategies. By exploring these top-performing ETFs, investors can gain insights into some of the most sought-after investment opportunities in the ETF universe.

SPDR S&P 500 ETF (SPY)

The SPDR S&P 500 ETF is one of the most widely recognized and heavily traded ETFs. It aims to track the performance of the S&P 500 Index, which represents the 500 largest publicly traded companies in the United States. Investing in SPY provides investors with broad exposure to the U.S. equity market, allowing them to participate in the performance of large-cap stocks across various sectors.

Vanguard Total Stock Market ETF (VTI)

The Vanguard Total Stock Market ETF seeks to replicate the performance of the CRSP US Total Market Index. This ETF provides investors with exposure to the entire U.S. stock market, including small-, mid-, and large-cap stocks.

VTI offers broad diversification and low expense ratios, making it an attractive option for investors looking for comprehensive U.S. equity exposure.

iShares Core S&P 500 ETF (IVV)

The iShares Core S&P 500 ETF is another popular ETF that aims to track the performance of the S&P 500 Index. IVV provides investors with broad exposure to large-cap U.S. stocks and is known for its low expense ratio. It is a suitable choice for investors seeking long-term growth potential and stability through exposure to established companies.

Invesco QQQ Trust (QQQ)

The Invesco QQQ Trust is an ETF that tracks the Nasdaq-100 Index, which includes 100 of the largest non-financial companies listed on the Nasdaq stock exchange. QQQ offers investors exposure to the technology, communication services, consumer discretionary, and healthcare sectors. It is particularly popular among investors interested in innovative and growth-oriented companies.

iShares Russell 2000 ETF (IWM)

The iShares Russell 2000 ETF seeks to track the performance of the Russell 2000 Index, which represents small-cap U.S. stocks. IWM provides investors with exposure to companies with smaller market capitalizations, offering the potential for higher growth and diversification beyond large-cap stocks.

Vanguard Total Bond Market ETF (BND)

The Vanguard Total Bond Market ETF is designed to track the performance of the Bloomberg Barclays U.S. Aggregate Float Adjusted Index, which represents the U.S. investment-grade bond market. BND offers investors exposure to a wide range of U.S. Treasury, corporate, and mortgage-backed securities, providing diversification and potential income generation.

iShares MSCI EAFE ETF (EFA)

The iShares MSCI EAFE ETF seeks to track the performance of

the MSCI EAFE Index, which represents developed market equities outside of the United States and Canada. EFA provides investors with exposure to companies in Europe, Australasia, and the Far East, offering diversification and the potential to participate in international market growth.

Vanguard FTSE Emerging Markets ETF (VWO)

The Vanguard FTSE Emerging Markets ETF aims to track the performance of the FTSE Emerging Markets All Cap China A Inclusion Index. VWO offers investors exposure to stocks of companies located in emerging markets, providing potential opportunities for higher returns but also higher volatility. It is an option for investors seeking diversification beyond developed markets.

iShares U.S. Real Estate ETF (IYR)

The iShares U.S. Real Estate ETF tracks the performance of the Dow Jones U.S. Real Estate Index, which represents the U.S. real estate sector. IYR offers investors exposure to companies engaged in real estate ownership, development, and management. This ETF can provide diversification and income potential through real estate investment trusts (REITs).

WisdomTree U.S. High Dividend Fund (DHS)

The WisdomTree U.S. High Dividend Fund focuses on dividend-paying stocks within the U.S. equity market. DHS aims to track the performance of the WisdomTree U.S. High Dividend Index, which selects stocks based on their dividend yields. This ETF is suitable for income-oriented investors seeking exposure to dividend-paying companies with the potential for consistent cash flow. The top 10 ETFs that provide investors with diverse investment opportunities. These ETFs cover various asset classes, including U.S. equities, international equities, bonds, real estate, and high dividend stocks. By understanding the features and objectives of these ETFs, investors can consider them as potential components of their investment portfolios. However, it's important to conduct further research and consider individual investment objectives, risk tolerance, and time horizon before making any investment decisions.

ETF Investing Strategies: Building a Successful Portfolio

In this final chapter of our journey through the intricate world of Exchange-Traded Funds (ETFs), we delve into the art of constructing a robust and diversified portfolio. The power of ETFs lies not only in their ability to provide exposure to a wide range of asset classes but also in their versatility as investment vehicles. By carefully selecting and combining various ETFs, investors can craft a portfolio that aligns with their risk tolerance, investment goals, and market outlook. Building a well-diversified portfolio is paramount for long-term success. Diversification allows investors to spread their risk across different asset classes, reducing the impact of individual security or sector volatility on overall portfolio performance. ETFs, with their broad exposure to multiple securities, offer a convenient and efficient way to achieve diversification within a single investment.

To construct a robust portfolio, it is essential to consider asset allocation, which involves determining the optimal distribution of investments across different asset classes, such as equities, fixed income, and commodities. This allocation should be based on factors such as risk tolerance, investment time horizon, and financial goals. ETFs play a crucial role in implementing asset allocation strategies, as they offer a diverse range of options to match different asset class exposures.

Another key consideration in portfolio construction is the selection of ETFs that align with specific investment themes or strategies. This allows investors to target specific sectors or investment themes that they believe will outperform the broader market. For example, an investor with a bullish view on technology stocks may choose to allocate a portion of their portfolio to a sector-specific ETF that tracks a technology index.

Moreover, investors can employ factor-based investing strategies using ETFs. Factors, such as value, growth, momentum, and quality, have been identified as drivers of stock returns. By selecting ETFs that focus on specific factors, investors can tilt their portfolios towards these desired characteristics, potentially

enhancing returns or managing risk.

ETF Investing Strategies: Building a Successful Portfolio

Now that we understand the importance of constructing a diversified portfolio, let us explore some popular ETF investing strategies that can help investors achieve their financial goals.

Core-Satellite Approach: This strategy combines the stability of a core portfolio of broad-based ETFs with the potential for higher returns through satellite positions in specialized or thematic ETFs. The core portion provides broad market exposure, while the satellite positions allow investors to express specific investment themes or capitalize on market opportunities.

Tactical Asset Allocation: This strategy involves dynamically adjusting the portfolio's asset allocation based on changing market conditions and economic outlook. ETFs make it easier to implement tactical asset allocation strategies, as they offer instant liquidity and flexibility to shift exposures across asset classes swiftly.

Dividend Investing: Dividend-focused ETFs target companies that consistently pay dividends or have a history of dividend growth. These ETFs allow investors to capture regular income streams while potentially benefiting from long-term capital appreciation.

Income Generation: Fixed income ETFs provide exposure to various types of bonds, including government bonds, corporate bonds, and municipal bonds. These ETFs offer investors the opportunity to generate regular income from coupon payments, making them suitable for income-focused portfolios.

Sustainable Investing: Environmental, Social, and Governance (ESG) ETFs focus on companies that meet specific sustainability criteria. These ETFs allow socially conscious investors to align their portfolios with their values while seeking potential financial returns.

Smart Beta Strategies: Smart beta ETFs seek to capture specific factors or investment strategies beyond traditional market-cap weighting. These strategies can include low volatility, high dividend yield, or fundamental weighting. Smart beta ETFs offer investors the potential to outperform traditional market-cap-weighted indices.

Global or International Exposure: ETFs provide convenient access to international markets, allowing investors to diversify geographically and capitalize on global investment opportunities. Global or international ETFs can offer exposure to developed markets, emerging markets, or specific regions or countries.

Risk Management: ETFs can be used as tools for risk management by hedging against specific risks or providing inverse exposure to markets or sectors. These ETFs can act as a form of insurance within a portfolio, mitigating potential losses during market downturns.

It is important to note that each of these strategies carries its own risks and considerations. Investors should conduct thorough research, analyze historical performance, and understand the underlying holdings and expense ratios of the ETFs they choose to include in their portfolios.

By combining different ETF investing strategies and tailoring them to individual investment objectives, risk tolerance, and time horizon, investors can build

portfolios that are designed to

weather market fluctuations,

capture growth opportunities, and

potentially achieve their financial

goals.

We have explored the art of constructing a robust and diversified portfolio using a range of ETF investing strategies. From core-satellite approaches to dividend investing, income generation, and sustainable investing, there are numerous strategies that investors can employ to align their portfolios with their unique investment goals.

The versatility and flexibility of ETFs make them ideal building blocks for constructing portfolios that suit individual preferences and risk profiles. Whether you are a conservative investor seeking steady income, a growth-oriented investor aiming for capital appreciation, or an investor with a specific market outlook, ETFs offer a wealth of opportunities to help you achieve your financial objectives.

As we conclude our journey through the world of ETFs, it is important to remember that successful investing requires careful planning, research, and continuous monitoring of market conditions.

By incorporating ETFs into your

investment toolkit and

implementing well-thought-out

strategies, you can unlock the

potential of these innovative

investment vehicles and embark on

a path toward financial success.

Now armed with a deep understanding of ETFs and their myriad possibilities, you are poised to navigate the ever-changing landscape of modern investing with confidence and precision. Embrace the world of ETF investing and unleash the power of your portfolio with "Mastering ETFs" your comprehensive guide to mastering the art of ETFs and achieving your

financial dreams.

Printed in Dunstable, United Kingdom